Science

The microscope symbol indicates a science project or activity, or where scientific information is given. These projects encourage investigating birds. If the symbol is green, it signals an environmental issue.

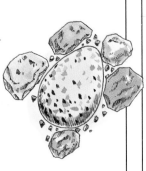

History

The key with the scroll and hourglass shows where historical information is given. These sections explore how people have viewed birds through the ages: as pest, pet, provider of eggs and feathers, and as inspiration to fly.

Maths

A ruler and compass indicate maths information and activities. Activities involve looking at shapes and sizes, comparing scale, and estimating how many birds are in a flock. All these projects improve an understanding of birds.

Arts, crafts, and music

The symbol showing a sheet of music and art tools signals art, crafts, and musical activities. These fun and informative projects include practical crafts, like building a nest box, and more creative activities, like reproducing bird songs.

CONTENTS

WHAT ARE BIRDS? 4/5

FEATHERS 6/7

FLIGHT..8/9

MIGRATION 10/11

BIRD BEAKS....................................12/13

FOOD AND FEEDING......................14/15

FEET..16/17

NIGHT BIRDS 18/19

BIRD COMMUNICATION...............20/21

COURTSHIP 22/23

NEST BUILDING 24/25

EGGS AND YOUNG 26/27

WHERE BIRDS LIVE........................28/29

THE VARIETY OF BIRDS......................30

GLOSSARY 31

INDEX..32

WHAT ARE BIRDS?

Birds are warm-blooded animals which breathe air. However, they also lay eggs and are the only animals in the world with feathers. All birds have wings, although some, such as penguins and ostriches, cannot fly. There are thought to be over 9,000 species of birds in the world. Scientists divide them into 27 orders, or groups. Over half of all birds belong to the order of perching birds.

Brilliantly coloured macaws live in noisy flocks in the world's rainforests. The species shown here are endangered in the wild.

Blue and yellow macaw

Scarlet macaw

The first birds
All living things change over thousands of years to improve their chances of survival. This process of change is called evolution. Birds evolved from reptiles about 150 million years ago. Their feathers developed from the scales which covered their ancestors. Wings gradually evolved from front legs. The **Archaeopteryx** first bird was the *Archaeopteryx* ("ancient wing"). It was about the size of a gull and had the sharp teeth of a lizard. It was a poor flier and used to climb trees and then glide away.

Legend and symbol
Birds have been so successful that they can be found virtually everywhere. Over the years, different cultures have come into contact with birds and attached various meanings to them. Bird flight has always inspired awe in earthbound humans. Birds have often been viewed as bearers of good fortune. However, crows, vultures and other carrion-scavenging birds are commonly associated with evil or horror.

The phoenix
This bird was worshipped in Ancient Egypt, but exists only in legend. The phoenix was said to set itself on fire and then rise from its own ashes.

The dove
The dove as a symbol of peace originated with the biblical story of Noah, who sent a dove from his Ark to find dry land.

FOCUS ON

BIRDS

ANITA GANERI

INTRODUCTION

Birds are the most plentiful of the earth's warm-blooded animals. Scientists have estimated that there may be over 100,000 million birds in the world altogether. Their success is largely due to their ability to fly, which gives them versatility in finding food and places to live. This book provides the science to understand birds, while linking them with history and literature, maths projects, geographical facts, and arts activities. The key below shows how the subjects are divided. We hope that the activities on the following pages help you develop your own ways of discovering birds.

This edition published 2003
© Aladdin Books Ltd 2003

Designed and produced by
Aladdin Books Ltd
28 Percy Street
London W1T 2BZ

First published in
Great Britain in 1992.
Watts Books
96 Leonard Street
London EC2A 4XD

ISBN 0 7496 5375 2

A catalogue record for this book is available from the British Library.

Printed in UAE

Design   David West Children's
                    Book Design
Designer   Flick Killerby
Series director   Bibby Whittaker
Editor   Elise Bradbury
Picture research   Emma Krikler
Illustrators   Rob Shone
                    Adrian Lascom,
                    Garden Studios

The author, Anita Ganeri, has written many books for children on natural history and other topics.

The educational consultant, Fiona Christie, has been a primary school teacher for several years in New Zealand and Britain.

The consultant, Sylvie Sullivan, is a freelance editor specialising in ornithology and natural history. She works part-time with the Royal Society for the Protection of Birds.

Geography
The symbol of the planet earth shows where geographical facts and activities are included. Because there is growing concern about the state of the environment, facts on green issues are highlighted with a green symbol.

Language and literature
An open book is the sign for information about language. These sections explore how words can be derived from the natural world around us. Activities also include examining how birds have inspired legends, poems, myths, and stories.

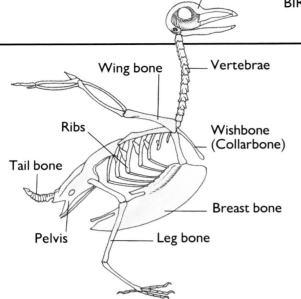

Skull

Wing bone — Vertebrae

Ribs

Wishbone (Collarbone)

Tail bone

Breast bone

Pelvis — Leg bone

Inside a bird

Birds are vertebrates, with an internal skeleton and backbone. Flying birds have very light skeletons, to reduce the amount of weight they have to carry in flight. Many of their bones are hollow. The inside of the bone looks like a honeycomb. Birds also have lightweight beaks, instead of heavy, bony jaws.

Bird records

There is an amazing variety of different bird species. Although all birds share similar body structure, they differ enormously in colour, size and shape. Some birds are so plentiful that they become pests. Others, like the California condor, are extremely rare.

Largest and smallest

The ostrich is the largest bird in the world. It can grow up to 2.7 m tall. The smallest bird is the bee hummingbird of Cuba, which is no larger than a bumble bee.

Ostrich

Most common

The domestic fowl, also known as the chicken, is the world's most common bird. In the wild, the red-billed quelea of Africa is the most numerous bird.

Scarlet macaw

Hyacinth macaw

The white stork

In Europe, the stork is a symbol of good luck. In legend, the stork delivers newborn babies to homes.

The pelican

The pelican got its reputation for being a dutiful parent in the Middle Ages (5-15th centuries). It was fabled to pierce its chest and feed its young with its blood.

Mute swan

Domestic fowl

Heaviest

The heaviest flying bird ever recorded was a mute swan that weighed 23 kg. The Kori bustard can also grow to this weight.

FEATHERS

All birds have feathers. A large bird like a swan has up to 25,000. Feathers come in a variety of shapes and sizes, depending on their function. Body, or contour, feathers give the bird its shape. Wing feathers help the bird to fly, while tail feathers are used for steering, balance and braking. The colour of the feathers is important for camouflage and courtship displays. A male and female bird of the same species often have differently coloured feathers (or plumage).

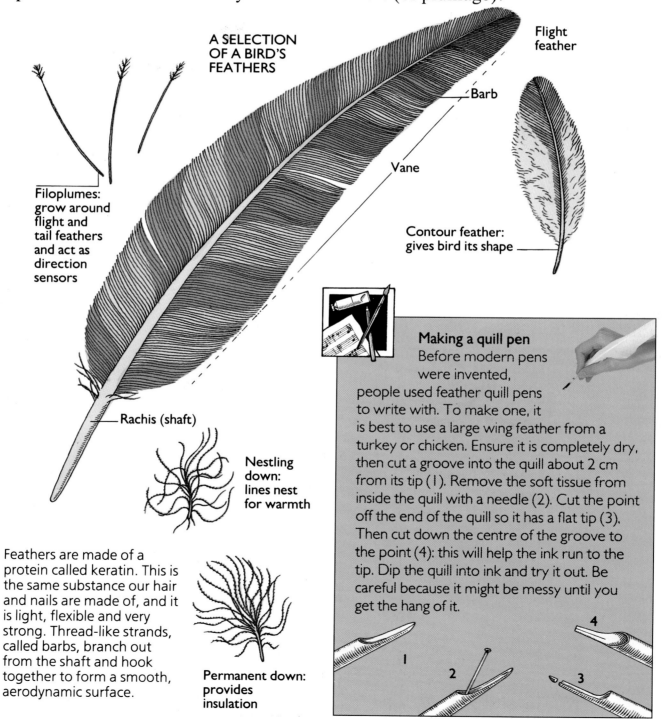

A SELECTION OF A BIRD'S FEATHERS

Flight feather

Barb

Vane

Contour feather: gives bird its shape

Filoplumes: grow around flight and tail feathers and act as direction sensors

Rachis (shaft)

Nestling down: lines nest for warmth

Feathers are made of a protein called keratin. This is the same substance our hair and nails are made of, and it is light, flexible and very strong. Thread-like strands, called barbs, branch out from the shaft and hook together to form a smooth, aerodynamic surface.

Permanent down: provides insulation

Making a quill pen
Before modern pens were invented, people used feather quill pens to write with. To make one, it is best to use a large wing feather from a turkey or chicken. Ensure it is completely dry, then cut a groove into the quill about 2 cm from its tip (1). Remove the soft tissue from inside the quill with a needle (2). Cut the point off the end of the quill so it has a flat tip (3). Then cut down the centre of the groove to the point (4): this will help the ink run to the tip. Dip the quill into ink and try it out. Be careful because it might be messy until you get the hang of it.

Pheasant having a dustbath

Keeping in condition

A bird's feathers can get damaged or dirty as they go about their activities. Feathers are vital for flying and keeping warm and dry, so birds must take great care of them. They preen ruffled feathers with their beaks to pull them back into shape. Some birds preen their feathers with their feet (see page 17). Birds also oil their feathers to keep them waterproof. The oil is made in a gland near their tails. They apply this oil with their beaks. To keep their feathers clean and free from lice and parasites, birds frequently bathe in water or dust.

Blending into the background

The colouring of many birds' plumage is for camouflage. This means that the feathers blend in with a bird's surroundings so it cannot be easily picked out by predators and eaten. In general, female birds have more subdued colouring than males because they are vulnerable when sitting on the nest. Stripes, blotches and speckles can make it difficult to see a bird when it is in its natural habitat. The feathers of certain birds even change colour to improve camouflage. In winter, the willow grouse is pure white in its snowy habitat. When summer arrives, it turns mainly brown like the grasses where it nests. The feathers of desert larks are perfectly matched to their sandy environment.

Desert lark

The feather in history

People have long used feathers for practical and ceremonial purposes. Small, soft down feathers from chickens and ducks have been used to fill pillows and quilts for hundreds of years. People have enjoyed the challenge of luring fish to their hooks with feathers designed to look like insects. Chinese fishermen are thought to have tied kingfisher feathers to their fish hooks as far back as 1000 BC. Worldwide, different cultures decorate themselves in feathers on special occasions. The Maasai of Kenya wear ostrich feather headdresses to show that they have been initiated as warriors. In the past, the Aztecs of Mexico (15th century) made headdresses from the feathers of the brightly coloured tropical quetzal. European fashion in the early 1900s included peacock feather fans and hats trimmed with feathers from egrets.

Down filling

Aztec shield

Maasai warrior

FLIGHT

The champions of the air, birds can fly faster and further than any other animals. This has given them a great advantage over other creatures, allowing them to exploit food sources far and wide and escape from danger. Birds fly in different ways. Albatrosses soar and glide on rising currents of air. Hummingbirds hover in front of flowers by beating their wings an incredible 90 times a second. Other birds flap their wings with powerful strokes.

Male Anna's hummingbird hovering

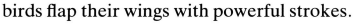

Laysan albatross braking in flight

Flapping flight
In this most common method of flight, huge muscles in the bird's breast contract to push the wing down. Then tendons act as pulleys and pull the wing back up.

Famous flight
The Ancient Greek legend of Icarus has been the subject of many paintings and poems. Icarus was the son of a brilliant inventor named Daedalus. Both were imprisoned on the island of Crete. Daedalus crafted two pairs of wings so they could escape. The wings worked well and Daedalus flew to freedom. However, Icarus enjoyed flying so much that he flew too close to the sun. The wax which attached his wings melted and Icarus plunged into the sea and drowned.

Icarus

Flightless birds
There are 10 families of flightless birds. Scientists believe that some flightless species, such as ostriches and emus, evolved from birds which were never able to fly because they were too heavy. But most of today's flightless birds are thought to have gradually lost the ability to fly because flight was not necessary to their survival. These species are mainly found on islands in the southern hemisphere where they had few natural predators. Unfortunately, when flightless birds came into contact with humans they had no defence or means of escape. The giant moa of New Zealand was an enormous flightless bird which grew up to 4 m tall. It was hunted to extinction by humans some 600 years ago.

Giant moa

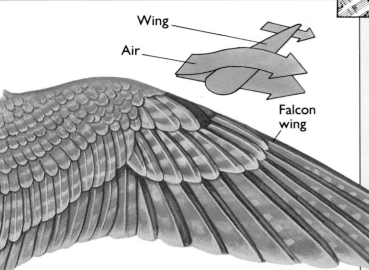

Wing

Air

Falcon wing

Flickbook flight

Animation is a sequence of pictures that, when passed quickly before the eyes, looks like it is moving. You can animate the flight pattern of a bird: swooping, flapping, bouncing or wheeling. Make a small notebook with blank pages. Choose a bird to illustrate and draw it in flight. On each page, draw the bird in its next stage of flying, like the examples below. When you have drawn each page, flick through the book quickly. The bird will look like it is flying.

A bird's whole body is designed for flight. Its wings are shaped like aerofoils, flat underneath and slightly curved from front to back on top. As the bird flies, air flows over its wing. As it does so, the aerofoil shape creates an area of high pressure under the wing and an area of low pressure above it. This pushes the wing, and the bird, upwards. This design is so successful that it is also used for aircraft wings.

Eagle

Chaffinch

Mallard

Flightless cormorant
There are many species of cormorants which can fly, but the flightless species lives only on the Galapagos Islands off the coast of Ecuador. Its small wings are useful when it dives for fish.

Kiwi
The kiwi of New Zealand is active only at night. It has no visible wings or tail. To get from place to place it breaks into a waddling run.

Penguins
Penguins slowly adapted from fliers to expert swimmers. This is because the icy lands of the southern hemisphere where they live are barren of life, but the ocean is full of food. Their wings act as flippers which help them to "fly" underwater.

Emu
The emu is an Australian bird which can grow to nearly 2 m. Like an ostrich, it has long, strong legs and feet which enable it to run at great speeds. Emus generally run at slower speeds so that they can travel long distances without tiring.

MIGRATION

Each autumn, many birds fly to warmer climates to escape the harsh winter weather and to find food. It is still a mystery how they find their way so accurately, to the same spot, year after year. Some seem to be guided by the sun, or by the stars and moon if they migrate at night. They also use geographical landmarks, such as rivers and mountains.

LONG DISTANCE FLIERS

Barnacle geese:
Arctic to
Europe

Arctic tern:
Arctic to
Antarctica

Sticking together
Geese and ducks are among the many birds which migrate in huge flocks. Geese fly in a V-formation, taking it in turns to lead.

Barn swallow:
Argentina to
Canada

Rufous hummingbird:
Mexico to Canada

Sooty shearwater:
Northern to southern oceans

Bobolink:
Argentina
to Canada

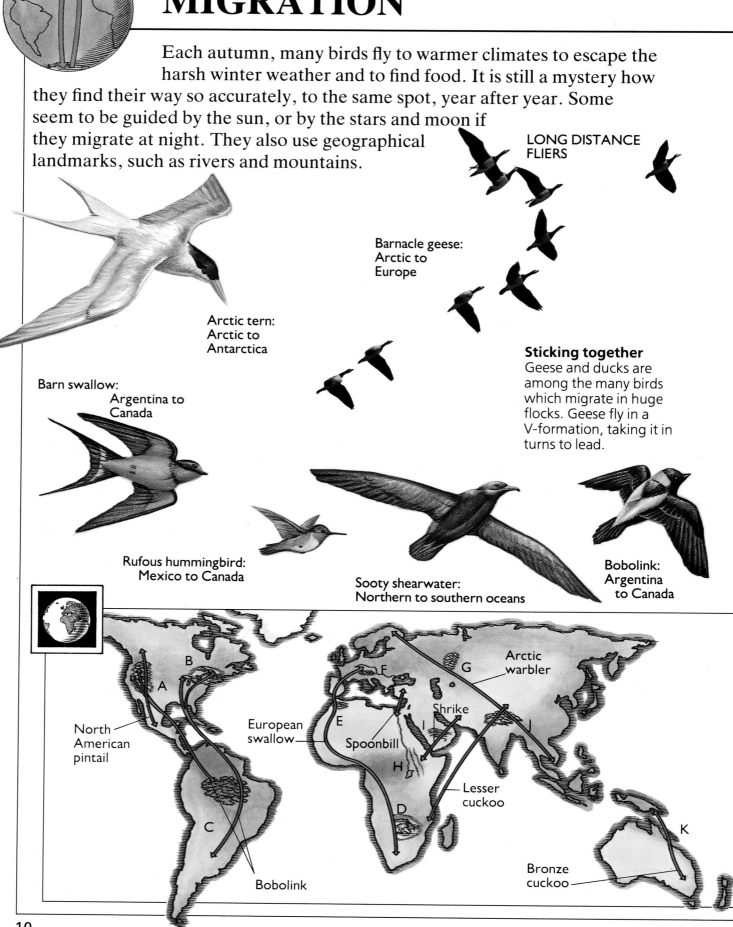

North
American
pintail

A

B

C

European
swallow

E

F

G

Arctic
warbler

Shrike

I

J

Spoonbill

H

D

Lesser
cuckoo

K

Bobolink

Bronze
cuckoo

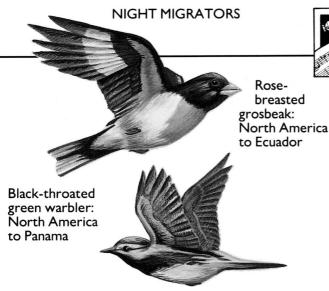

Rose-breasted grosbeak: North America to Ecuador

Black-throated green warbler: North America to Panama

Amazing journeys

Some migratory birds make extremely long journeys. The Arctic tern flies from the Arctic to the Antarctic and back every year – a round trip of over 40,000 km. In this way, it spends summer at each end of the Earth.

Most birds fly below 100 m when they migrate. Bar-headed geese, however, have to fly over the Himalayas, at a height of 8,000 m.

Count a flock

Some birds migrate alone, but many travel in large flocks. A flock of starlings can have up to a million birds. Try to estimate how many birds are in a passing flock.

Migration landmarks

Migrating birds rely heavily on familiar landmarks to find their way. This map shows some species which fly over famous landmarks on their journey from their summer breeding grounds to their winter feeding sites. Compare the migration paths of some other birds with a map and name the places they fly over.

A. Rocky Mountains
B. Niagara Falls
C. Amazonia
D. Victoria Falls
E. Atlas Mountains
F. The Alps
G. Ural Mountains
H. River Nile
I. Arabian Desert
J. The Himalayas
K. Great Barrier Reef

Survival game

Migrating birds face many hazards. The flights are often long and tiring. Dangers on the journey include fierce storms, predators, accidents or starvation. Experience the risks yourself by making a migration game. Make the game from card, as below. Starting at north, south, east or west, the object of the game is to get back to this position, moving clockwise. Roll the dice and move your bird. If it lands on red, take a card and follow its directions. If the bird lands on amber, it is safe for this turn. Take another turn if your bird lands on a green square.

Dice

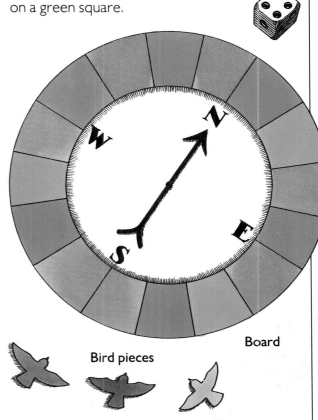

Board

Bird pieces

Penalty cards

TIRED WING REST FO 1 GO

BAD STORM MISS 2 GOES

Think of all the hazards migrating birds face, and write these on separate cards. Each card should carry a penalty as well. A card is taken when a player lands on red.

BIRD BEAKS

Birds have tough, lightweight beaks (also called bills) which they use for catching, breaking open or holding onto food. They also use their beaks for preening (see page 7) and for building nests. Some birds' beaks serve more specialised functions. Bee-eaters excavate nest-holes in sandbanks with their beaks. The size and shape of a bird's beak depends on what it eats and where it finds its food. The tiny sword-billed hummingbird's slender bill is longer than its body. Its shape allows the bird to reach nectar deep inside forest flowers.

Giant toucan

Toucans live in South American rainforests. A toucan's huge bill allows it to reach for fruit. The function of the hornbill's amazing bill is not known for certain, but it might help other birds identify it. Hornbills are spread throughout Asia and Africa.

Hornbill

Can birds smell?
Most birds have a very poor sense of smell. The nostrils on their beaks are used to breathe. However, certain species have a keen nose. The kiwi has poor eyesight and feeds in darkness, so it has to rely on smell to find food. Its nostrils are at the tip of its long beak, which it sticks into the ground. There it can sniff out the earthworms it eats.

Kiwi

Looking for clues
Birds use their beaks to prise seeds from their husks, crack open nuts and peck at fruit. Look for the remains they leave behind to locate where birds have been feeding.

Male eclectus parrot

Not just for looks

Many beaks have special features for dealing with specific types of food or for particular functions. Parrots have hooked beaks for cracking open large nuts and seeds. Their beaks are also useful for climbing. Avocets use their long, slim bills to whisk through mud or deep water for food. Spoonbills swing their large, flat beaks from side to side in the water to catch food.

Avocet

Spoonbill

Lessons from nature

Birds have been adopted into language in many ways, for example in proverbs. Proverbs are sayings which teach a lesson or give advice. They often originate from observations of the natural world. If someone says "The early bird catches the worm", it means if you want something, you should get there before others. This proverb was inspired by birds that dig up worms at dawn. Another saying which uses birds to give advice is "Don't count your chickens before they've hatched", meaning don't take something for granted before it has happened. This observation refers to the fact that a bird's eggs are vulnerable, and some might be destroyed before the chicks hatch. What other expressions contain references to birds?

Birds under threat

The main threat to birds is the destruction of their habitats to grow crops, ranch cattle, expand cities and build tourist resorts. People further endanger birds by polluting wild places. Pollution occurs when something gets into the environment in such large quantities that it threatens life. Many bird species live near water which factories have contaminated with chemicals. Polychlorinated biphenyls (PCBs), extremely toxic chemicals used in the electrical industry, are believed to have poisoned this cormorant (below), resulting in its deformed beak. Litter is also a hazard for birds. Plastic and metal objects can get caught around their beaks when they poke through rubbish looking for food. Feeding then becomes difficult or impossible, and the birds can starve to death.

FOOD AND FEEDING

Birds have to eat regularly to get the huge amounts of energy they need for flying, nesting and egg laying. This energy can come from a wide variety of foods, such as plants, fruit, seeds, insects, worms and fish. Some birds will only eat one kind of food, while others, like starlings, feed on almost anything. A bird's diet depends on where it lives and what food is available. All birds spend a large part of their lives looking for food. The smaller a bird is, the more food it needs for its size, just to stay alive.

Flamingos feed with their heads held upside down in the water. As their beaks fill up with water, bristles catch tiny shrimps and water plants which they swallow for food.

Great frigatebird

Some birds do not find their own food. They steal it instead. Among these pirates are the frigatebirds. They fly after other seabirds and harass them into dropping their catch of fish in mid-air. Then the frigatebirds swoop and dive to catch the food before it lands in the sea.

Greater flamingo

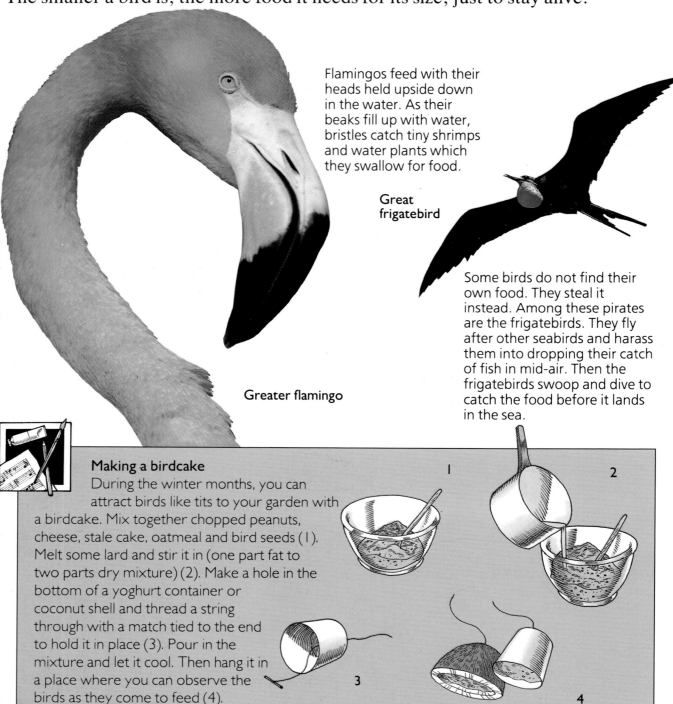

Making a birdcake
During the winter months, you can attract birds like tits to your garden with a birdcake. Mix together chopped peanuts, cheese, stale cake, oatmeal and bird seeds (1). Melt some lard and stir it in (one part fat to two parts dry mixture) (2). Make a hole in the bottom of a yoghurt container or coconut shell and thread a string through with a match tied to the end to hold it in place (3). Pour in the mixture and let it cool. Then hang it in a place where you can observe the birds as they come to feed (4).

1

2

3

4

DIFFERENT BEAKS FOR DIFFERENT FOODS

Sunbird: nectar	Finch: seeds	Vulture: carnivorous	Bluejay: omnivorous	Flycatcher: insects

Birds have adaptations which allow them to eat particular types of food. They have no teeth to chew their food. Instead, they have a special muscular chamber in their stomachs where food is ground up. Some birds swallow stones and grit to help this process along. The shape of the beak is also suited for different foods. Vultures have sharp beaks for tearing meat. Their heads and necks are bare, otherwise their feathers would get soaked in blood.

When they feed, birds swallow things which they cannot digest. These may include bones, fur, hard seed cases, shells and feathers. Some kinds of birds choke these up through their beaks as tightly-packed pellets, once or twice a day. Owls and many other birds, such as magpies and wading birds, produce pellets. Owl pellets are usually found under trees. If you take them apart, you can sometimes see what type of food a bird has been eating.

Dining out
Birds and products from birds are staple foods in most countries. Nearly every culture eats eggs from chickens, ducks or geese, and some cultures eat eggs from other kinds of birds. Collecting wild birds' eggs is illegal in most countries, but scientists have sampled the eggs of some species to find the best tasting egg. Chickens' eggs were deemed the best, while the worst tasting was the egg of the black tit. One Chinese delicacy is bird's nest soup. This speciality is made from the nests of a nocturnal species of swift from Sarawak. During the day the birds sleep in dark caves. Nesthunters search them out, and throw out the eggs and nestlings to collect the nests to sell. This has endangered the species.

Fried egg

Sarawak swiftlet in nest

Birds as pests
For centuries, farmers have used scarecrows to prevent seed-eating birds from devouring crops. Originally they were made from sticks and old clothes. Some modern scarecrows are mechanical. They move back and forth and emit loud noises and flashing lights to scare birds away.

Driven to extinction
The now extinct passenger pigeon was a common pest for farmers in the United States in the 1870s. As its forest habitat in the northeast of the country was cleared for farmland, the passenger pigeon began to feed on crops. The farmers' response was to shoot the adults and take the chicks from their nests. In 1914 the last of these birds was killed.

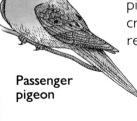

Passenger pigeon

FEET

Apart from walking and running, birds also use their feet for gripping and tearing food, climbing, swimming and preening their feathers. Most birds have three or four toes on each foot, but the exact size and shape of their feet depends on their lifestyle. The partridge spends most of its time on the ground, so it needs strong feet which are good for running and scratching for food. When perching birds roost on branches at night, their toes lock around the branch so they do not fall off.

For running
Ostriches have only two toes on each foot. These are highly specialised for fast running. Ostriches cannot fly, but they can run at up to 70 km/h for short distances.

Ostrich foot

Coot foot

For balance
The African jacana, or lily trotter, has toes about 8 cm long – the longest of any bird. These enable it to spread its weight over its feet so it can walk across waterlily leaves without sinking.

African jacana walking on lily leaf

Mallard foot

For swimming
Ducks and geese have large, webbed feet which act as paddles when they swim, and as brakes when they land on water. Coots have lobes of skin between their toes. These help in swimming and stop the coot from sinking into mud.

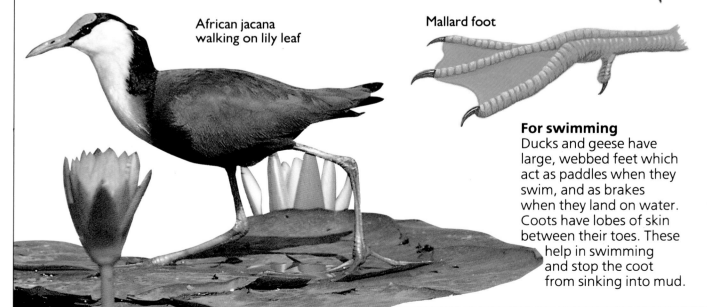

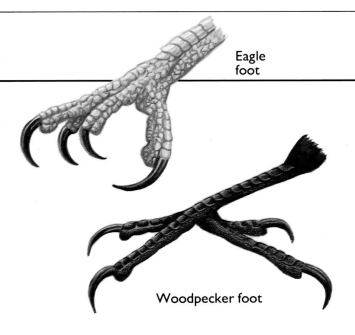

Eagle foot

Woodpecker foot

For gripping

Eagles and other birds of prey have sharp, curved talons on their feet for holding and tearing meat. Their legs and feet are very strong, but these birds find walking difficult because their talons are so long. The long-clawed feet of woodpeckers are designed for climbing tree trunks. They have two toes pointing forwards and two backwards.

Claws for combing

To keep their feathers clean and tidy, birds preen them with their beaks and feet. Herons and bitterns specialise in using their feet to preen. They feed on eels, which makes their feathers slimy. To remove the slime, some of the feathers on the breast disintegrate into a powder which they rub into their dirty feathers. The heron then "combs" off the slime with tiny teeth on the middle claws of its feet. Nightjars are nocturnal birds which feed on a diet of moths and other insects. They also have comb-like central claws to clean moth scales off their feathers.

Heron claw

Bittern claw

Great blue heron preening

Plastercasting bird prints

Before you set out to find a footprint of a bird to plastercast, first collect the following materials: a small tin, a stick, stiff paper, paper clips, plaster of paris, water, clear varnish and a knife. When you select a bird print, stand a 3 cm-wide strip of paper in a circle around the footprint (1). Fasten it together with a paper clip. Mix the plaster of paris in a tin with water, stirring with your stick. Add water until the mixture is thick but can still be poured. Then pour the mixture into the paper ring, until the area is evenly covered (2). Leave the plaster to dry for 10 – 15 minutes. Then prise the cast loose with a knife and clean off the mud and grass. In 24 hours when the cast is completely solid, carefully clean and varnish it (3). Compare the print with a bird identification book to see if you can find out what kind of bird made it.

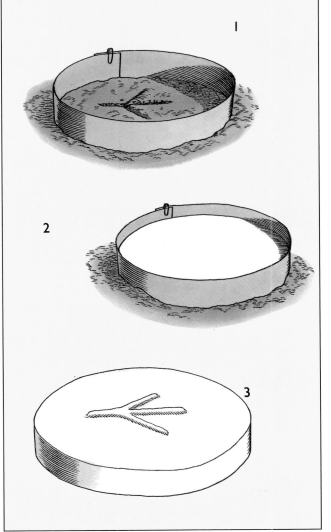

1

2

3

NIGHT BIRDS

Most birds are active during the day. Only a very few are nocturnal, and most of these are owls. Night birds have special features, for instance exceptional hearing or vision, to help them find their way around and to locate food in the dark. Being nocturnal has several advantages. There are fewer competitors for food and fewer predators to be attacked by.

Echo off wall warns bird not to fly into it

Oilbird makes clicking noises

Like bats, oilbirds of South America use echo-location to find their way around the dark caves where they live. They make clicking sounds which hit solid objects, such as cave walls. The returning echoes tell the oilbirds in which direction to fly.

Owls

Owls are perfectly designed for hunting at night. The adaptations which make them so successful give owls their unique appearance. They have huge eyes and superb eyesight for spotting their prey of small mammals and birds. Owls also have excellent hearing for locating prey. Their slit-like ears are hidden behind feathers, but you can see the oval facial disks which act like earflaps to channel sound into the ears. One ear is often higher and bigger than the other, for pinpointing sounds even more accurately. Once they have located their prey, owls can swoop silently down and take it by surprise. Fringed feathers and feathered legs and feet help to muffle any sound.

Down under

New Guinea, Australia and New Zealand are home to some of the world's most unusual nocturnal birds. The rare kakapo, a flightless owl-like parrot, lives in the forests of New Zealand. Another odd night bird of this region is the frogmouth. It feeds at night, mainly on insects. During the day the frogmouth rests on a branch with its beak pointed up to the sky. Its colours and body position camouflage it to look like a broken branch.

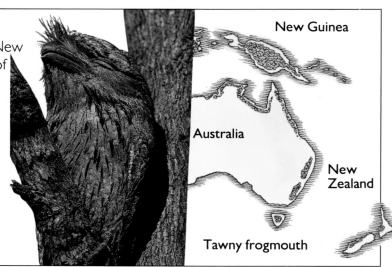

New Guinea

Australia

New Zealand

Tawny frogmouth

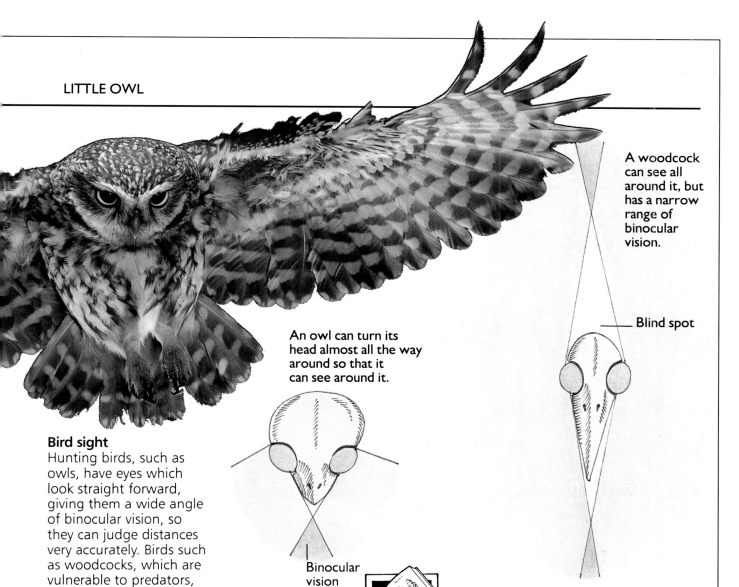

A woodcock can see all around it, but has a narrow range of binocular vision.

Blind spot

An owl can turn its head almost all the way around so that it can see around it.

Binocular vision

Bird sight
Hunting birds, such as owls, have eyes which look straight forward, giving them a wide angle of binocular vision, so they can judge distances very accurately. Birds such as woodcocks, which are vulnerable to predators, have eyes at the side of the head. They can see all around them.

During daylight hours
Nocturnal birds have to find a safe place to rest when daylight comes. At night their enemies are asleep, but daytime is dangerous; they might be attacked if they are noticed. Night birds usually have brown, grey and beige feathers to blend in with their surroundings. Owls roost in barns or tree trunks for protection. The nightjar and the woodcock spend the day resting on the ground, sitting perfectly still. Their dull, mottled plumage keeps them very well camouflaged.

Nightjar

Night birds and words
The best known nocturnal birds are owls. In many cultures owls are viewed as wise. Athena, the mythical Greek goddess of wisdom, is often portrayed with an owl. Native American legends also attribute owls with powerful, sometimes supernatural, forces. These legends claim that owls are messengers of death. A A Milne sees owls in a very different way. His book, *Winnie the Pooh*, features a conceited but harmless owl who thinks he is much more intelligent than he actually is. Another bird which has inspired many writers is the nightingale. It is active during the day, but also sings throughout the night. The English poet, John Keats (1795-1821), wrote a famous poem called *Ode to a Nightingale*, describing the bird's beautiful night song. Try writing a verse or story about a bird you find inspiring.

BIRD COMMUNICATION

Birds have various ways of communicating with each other. They use their voices in calls and songs. These are used to establish and defend territory, as warnings, to identify other birds in a group, and in courtship. Some birds use visual signals to send messages. They may fly in a special way or make certain movements to communicate. Even a bird's colouring can send a message. Flocks of migrating geese, for example, keep together by following the white rump of the bird in front.

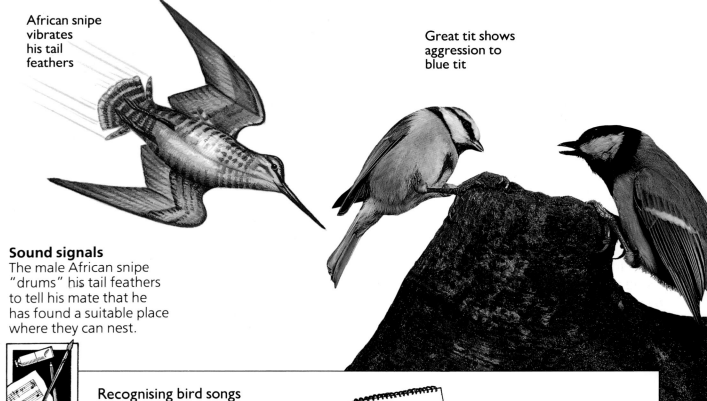

African snipe vibrates his tail feathers

Great tit shows aggression to blue tit

Sound signals
The male African snipe "drums" his tail feathers to tell his mate that he has found a suitable place where they can nest.

Recognising bird songs
Birds make a variety of chirps, clucks and other noises to communicate with each other. In addition, many species have a certain song they sing to protect their territories. Good bird watchers can recognise a species by the song it sings. Recognising bird songs takes a lot of practice. The best time to listen is early morning or dusk. Bring a notebook, and when you hear a bird sing, try to describe the call it makes or reproduce the melody. For example, chiff-chaffs make a sound that sounds like their name. After time, when you become familiar with certain songs, you will be able to identify the calls of different species.

CHIRJ-TI-TEW
WISYOO
TYO-TO

Yellowhammer singing

You may be able to reproduce certain bird songs by whistling. If possible, get a record of bird songs which will help you to identify them.

Keeping in contact

Some birds can recognise each other's voices. Seabirds and penguins nest in huge colonies of thousands of birds. Gannets, for example, are seabirds which nest very close together in large groups. While one bird sits on the egg, its mate must go in search of food to bring back. When it returns to the colony, it gives a loud call to announce that it has returned. Its partner recognises its voice, and guides it to the nest by calling back.

Talking birds

People have been keeping birds as pets for centuries. The most popular are birds in the parrot family, including cockatoos and macaws, which can mimic other noises, particularly human speech. African grey parrots are the most accomplished at this. Sadly, the popularity of talking birds as pets has taken its toll on several species. Many birds caught for the pet trade are killed or injured when they are captured. More die when they are transported to other countries. Some species have become very rare as a result.

Comparing voices

Human speech is made in a different way than bird sounds. In humans, the vocal cords are located high in the throat. When we speak, we breathe out air which passes over these cords and makes them vibrate. This produces sound, which is then altered by our nasal cavities and the way we move our lips, tongue, cheeks and teeth. A bird has no vocal cords. Its voice box, located at the bottom of the windpipe, makes sound. Tiny muscles in the voice box move to create all the different sounds a bird can make. Birds do not use their tongues or cheeks to alter the sounds the voice box produces. This is why a bird can sing with its beak closed. Although humans inherit the ability to produce sound, a child learns speech from the people around it. In contrast to this, bird chicks inherit the song of their species and then copy slight variations of it from other birds.

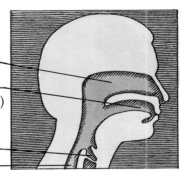

HUMAN

Nasal cavity affects voice

Tongue changes sound

Larynx (voice box) and vocal cords together create sound

Windpipe

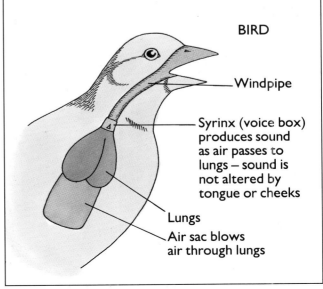

BIRD

Windpipe

Syrinx (voice box) produces sound as air passes to lungs – sound is not altered by tongue or cheeks

Lungs

Air sac blows air through lungs

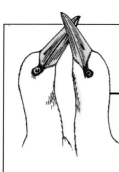

COURTSHIP

Birds need to find a suitable partner to mate with and breed. The male birds usually do the chasing, and competition among them is fierce. They have various ways of wooing females. Some show off their nest-building or hunting skills, or give displays of dancing and singing. Some adopt more colourful feathers just for the breeding season. Puffins even grow more colourful beaks, which moult when the season is over.

Impressive pouch
Male frigatebirds have bright red pouches of skin on their throats. To attract a female, they inflate these like giant balloons, sometimes for several hours. When a female bird chooses her mate, she rubs her head against his pouch.

Ruff

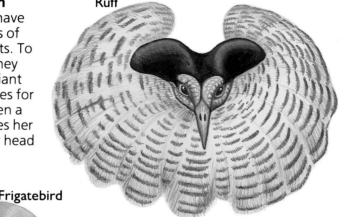

Frigatebird

Attractive feathers
Male ruffs perform their courtship display on communal grounds, called leks. Males defend a small patch, where they can show their feathers.

Good provider
Some male birds, like this British robin, bring the female a gift of food. This shows her whether the male is going to be a good provider of food.

Robin

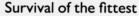

Survival of the fittest
Male birds of different species have a wide variety of ways to attract a mate. These range from the beautiful plumage of a peacock to the elegant dance of a riflebird. The reason for courtship displays is that the males need to impress prospective mates. If a male's appearance or display is effective in attracting females, he will be able to pass on the characteristics which made him successful. In this way, traits which help an animal reproduce gradually spread to the whole species. This is one aspect of evolution.

Charles Darwin was the British naturalist who developed the theory of evolution in the 1850s.

This female riflebird is wooed each year by the male's amazing dance.

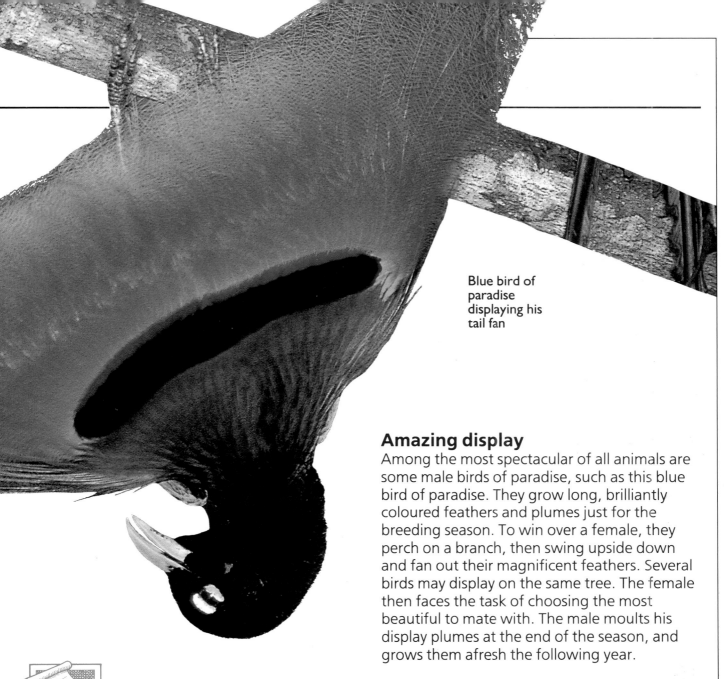

Blue bird of
paradise
displaying his
tail fan

Amazing display

Among the most spectacular of all animals are
some male birds of paradise, such as this blue
bird of paradise. They grow long, brilliantly
coloured feathers and plumes just for the
breeding season. To win over a female, they
perch on a branch, then swing upside down
and fan out their magnificent feathers. Several
birds may display on the same tree. The female
then faces the task of choosing the most
beautiful to mate with. The male moults his
display plumes at the end of the season, and
grows them afresh the following year.

Attracting attention

For hundreds of years, native peoples of
New Guinea have decorated themselves in
the courtship display feathers of birds of paradise to
make themselves more attractive. Elaborate feather
headdresses are worn in tribal dances to impress
members of the opposite sex. Although many birds
were killed for this tradition, birds of paradise were
not under serious threat until 1522 when Europeans
caught their first glimpse of one brought back on a
Spanish trading ship. By the end of the 19th century,
bird of paradise feathers were in such demand for
European fashion that the birds began to decline
seriously. They are now protected and most species
are slowly recovering their numbers.

New
Guinea
tribesman

NEST-BUILDING

The majority of birds lay their eggs in nests. These provide safe, warm places where the eggs can hatch and the chicks can be raised. Plants, twigs, mud and feathers are among the most common nest-building materials, but nests of more bizarre materials, like barbed wire, have also been found. Nests range from the tiny, thimble-sized cups of hummingbirds to the great platforms of sticks built by eagles.

Red-headed weaver
building nest

Skilled craftsman

To build his nest, the male village weaver of Africa starts by knotting a blade of grass round a twig. He may have to try this several times before he is successful. Next he weaves in more grass and leaves to form a ball-shaped nest. Hundreds of male weaver birds may build their nests in the same tree. When a male completes his nest, he advertises it by hanging upside down from it and flapping his wings. A female then inspects the nest and will only move in if she is satisfied with what she finds.

The cuckoo imposter

The female European cuckoo never builds a nest of her own, nor does she raise her own chicks. Instead she selects another bird's nest which contains eggs, and in it lays one of her own. This egg is patterned to look very similar to the eggs already in the nest, so the parent birds do not notice it and incubate it with the rest. After 12 days, the cuckoo chick hatches, often camouflaged to look like the other nestlings. It pushes the other chicks out of the nest so it receives all the food the parent birds bring back. It grows larger and larger until it is far bigger than its foster parents.

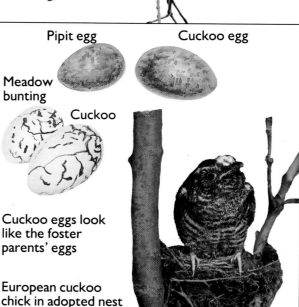

Pipit egg

Cuckoo egg

Meadow bunting

Cuckoo

Cuckoo eggs look like the foster parents' eggs

European cuckoo chick in adopted nest

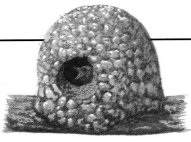

Rufous ovenbird
Rufous ovenbirds build great, spherical nests with a cement of mud, grass and hair. The nests get their name from old-fashioned ovens.

Puffin
Puffins nest in colonies on clifftops. They lay their eggs in burrows, which they have either dug themselves or taken over from other animals.

Tailorbird
To make their nests, tailorbirds use strands of cobweb to sew together leaves still attached to a tree. They use their beaks as sewing needles.

Shapes in nature
Shapes are not just abstract geometrical symbols. They are everywhere in nature. Swallows make triangular nests of mud in corners. Many birds, like the reed warbler, weave almost spherical nests. The ovenbird builds a mud sphere to nest in. A sand martin digs cylindrical tunnels for its nest. Teardrop-shaped nests are made by the weaverbird. Think of the nests that different species build and describe their shapes.

Building a nest box
A nest box is an ideal way to attract birds to your garden. Birds which nest in holes, like great tits, will rear their young in nest boxes. To build one you will need a length of wood 150 cm long, 15 cm wide and 1 cm thick, an old inner tube or leather, two hooks and eyes, 24 nails 3.5 cm long, a saw, a brace and a bit (diameter 28 mm). Cut the length of wood as shown below. Using the brace and bit, make a hole in the front. Nail the 25 cm-length sides to the back and then the front to the 20 cm-length sides. Nail on the base. Nail the strip of leather or inner tube to the roof and to the back of the box so the leather forms a hinge. Fit on a hook and eye to keep the roof fastened. Hang the nest box where it can be seen from a window, but ensure that is at least 3 m above the ground so that predators cannot get in.

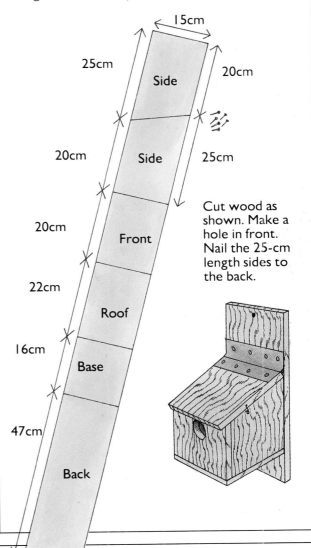

15cm

25cm — Side — 20cm

20cm — Side — 25cm

20cm — Front

22cm — Roof

16cm — Base

47cm — Back

Cut wood as shown. Make a hole in front. Nail the 25-cm length sides to the back.

EGGS AND YOUNG

Like their reptile ancestors, all types of birds lay eggs. But the number and colour of the eggs varies a great deal. Emperor penguins lay just one egg a season. Mallee fowl, on the other hand, lay up to 35 eggs a year. The colour of the eggs depends on where they are laid and how much camouflage they need. The young bird develops inside the egg, where it has a store of food and a supply of air.

A CHICKEN 10 DAYS AFTER FERTILISATION

Embryo

Eye

Yolk

Membrane: allows passage of air to embryo through pores of shell

Shell

Blood vessels bring nutrients to embryo

Inside the egg
The albumen and yolk provide the embryo with food for growth. The albumen, or white, supplies proteins, water and vitamins. It is transparent and difficult to see. The yolk supplies protein and fat.

Egg variation
Some birds, snakes and mammals feed on eggs. For this reason, eggs must be concealed or camouflaged so that they are not destroyed. The egg of every bird species is different. Egg size depends on how big the bird which produced it is. In some species, chicks stay in the egg longer before they hatch. These eggs have to be relatively large to contain the extra food needed for the chick to develop. The number of eggs a bird lays also depends on the species. If the chance of survival is good, the number of eggs is low. Otherwise, some species may lay many eggs, or replace eggs which are lost.

Plover eggs
Most species of plovers live on open ground and have to make their nests out in the open. Their eggs are patterned to look like their surroundings.

Owl eggs
Owls conceal their eggs in a nest, hole or a hollow tree, so their eggs do not need to be camouflaged. Most species have round, pure white eggs. Normally 2-6 eggs are laid at a time.

Hatching

Eggs need to be kept at a temperature of about 35°C, so that the chicks develop properly. The female usually sits on the eggs, keeping them warm with a bare area of skin on her breast. This incubation period lasts from just ten days for woodpecker chicks to almost 80 days for some albatrosses. Then the chick must break out of its shell. It uses its egg tooth, a bony knob on its beak, to crack the shell. The egg tooth later falls off. The length of time it takes a chick to hatch varies from species to species. Some chicks hatch in less than an hour. Albatross chicks may take six days.

Testing shell strength

Eggshells have to be quite strong to protect the chick as it develops. Test their strength with this experiment. You will need a plastic bottle with its bottom cut off, a beaker, a broken eggshell from a chicken, and sand. Place the shell round end up in a container. Rest the neck of the bottle on the shell and slowly add sand to the bottle. Continue this until the weight of the sand breaks the shell. Note the amount of sand used and try again with another shell. Do all shells break at the same weight?

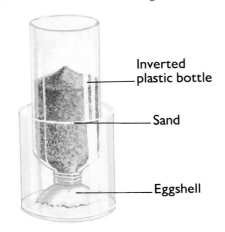

Inverted plastic bottle

Sand

Eggshell

Comparing size

One of the ways we understand size is by looking at objects in relation to one another. Although the illustration below does not show the actual size of the eggs, because we are familiar with the size of a hen's egg we can estimate the size of the other bird's eggs. This is known as showing proportion.

Ostrich

Hen

Hummingbird

Guillemot egg

These sea birds make no nest, but lay their eggs on cliff ledges. One end is pointed, which causes the egg to turn in a circle rather than roll off the edge.

Little tern egg

Terns live near water and often nest on beaches. Their 2-4 eggs are sand-coloured with dark specks. They are patterned to look like rocks on a seaweed-strewn shore.

WHERE BIRDS LIVE

With their adaptations for flight and feeding, birds are able to live all over the world. Their habitats range from the freezing poles to the baking deserts, and from rushing rivers to steamy jungles. Flight has given them the mobility to exploit a wide variety of food supplies and habitats. Being warm-blooded, they also have the advantage of maintaining a constant body temperature and staying active whatever the weather.

Antarctica

The 16 species of penguin all live in the southern hemisphere. Six species, including these emperor penguins, are even found in Antarctica itself, despite the extremely cold temperatures and wind. Emperors are the largest of all penguin species. They grow to just under one metre tall.

The tropics

About two-thirds of all species of birds live in the world's tropical rainforests. They include trogons and parrots. Rainforest birds are often brightly coloured. The bright green feathers of this rainbow lorikeet blend in with the foliage. Even its colourful markings could be mistaken for flowers or fruits in the lush forest.

Bird watching

The best places to observe birds are parks, gardens or woodland areas. Sit very quietly and try to keep out of sight. In a forest you will see that different species prefer a particular part of the woodland. Some birds will feed on the ground, others might nest among shrubs and some will sing from tree branches. Watch patiently and note down the colours, shape and behaviour of different types of birds, and where and when you saw them.

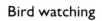

Desert

Roadrunners live in the North and Central American deserts. They rarely fly, but can race at great speeds after their prey – insects, lizards and snakes. They survive the scorching heat of the desert by staying in the shade until dusk when the air and ground cool off.

Mountains

Some birds of prey, like this golden eagle, soar above high mountains. They glide on rising currents of air, keeping a look out for prey below. They nest on cliff faces where they can rear their eaglets, protected from predators.

Never disturb nests or harm birds or eggs.

Keep a scrapbook to record the birds you see. Later you can compare it with a bird identification book.

National birds

Birds can be found virtually all over the world. Many nations have adopted as symbols birds which are native to the country or which migrate through the region. Often they are chosen for their beauty, rarity or some other special feature. Some birds have even been incorporated onto national flags or emblems. Can you think of any other ways in which birds have been used as symbols?

Australia

The black swan of Australia is revered as it is one of only three swan species in the southern hemisphere. It is all black with white wing feathers and a red bill.

Papua New Guinea

The flag of this country carries the silhouette of a bird of paradise, which is native to New Guinea. These birds are famed for their dazzling plumage and courtship displays.

The United States

The bald eagle was adopted as the national emblem of the United States in 1782. It was chosen because it is such a powerful, noble-looking bird.

Egypt

Egypt's national flag shows a bird of prey, which symbolises strength. Kestrels were held sacred in Ancient Egypt, and were often mummified.

Uganda

The national flag of Uganda in East Africa shows an African balearic crane, also known as a crowned crane. They are residents of this region and are held in special regard because of their striking appearance and amazing dance.

THE VARIETY OF BIRDS

Scientists classify birds into groups that share similar characteristics, like appearance and behaviour. All birds belong to the animal kingdom under the class "Aves." This class is divided into 27 orders (shown below), the orders into 174 families, families into genera and the genera into over 9,000 species. The chart below shows a typical bird from each order, identified in italics by the illustration. The number in brackets shows how many species are in the order. One order is broken down into species.

ORDERS (not to scale)

Struthioniformes (1)
Ostrich

Rheiformes (2)
Rheas, *Common rhea*

Casuariiformes (5)
Cassowaries, Emus, *Emu*

Apterygiformes (3)
Kiwis, *Common kiwi*

Tinamiformes (47)
Tinamous, *Great tinamou*

Podicipediformes (21)
Grebes, *Great crested grebe*

Ciconiiformes (117)
Storks, Herons, Egrets, Ibises, Spoonbills, *Snowy egret*

Sphenisciformes (18)
Penguins, *Emperor penguin*

Pelecaniformes (62)
Cormorants, Pelicans, Gannets, *Blue-footed booby*

Dinornithiformes (151)
Ducks, Swans, Geese, *Mallard duck*

Procellariiformes (104)
Albatrosses, Petrels, Shearwaters, *Black-footed albatross*

Gruiformes (209)
Coots, Moorhens, Crakes, Cranes, *Black coot*

Galliformes (268)
Fowls, Pheasants, Partridges, Grouse, Turkeys, Guineas, *Plumed quail*

Charadriiformes (331)
Gulls, Curlews, Snipes, Sandpipers, Woodcocks, Guillemots, *Ivory gull*

Falconiformes (288)
Kestrels, Eagles, Hawks Buzzards, Vultures, Kites, *Osprey*

Cuculiformes (143)
Cuckoos, Hoatzins, Roadrunners, *Great-spotted cuckoo*

Columbiformes (303)
Pigeons, Doves, *Rock dove*

Trogoniformes (37)
Trogons, *Quetzal*

Strigiformes (146)
Little owls, Barn owls, Tawny owls, Eagle owls, *Snowy owl*

Psittaciformes (340)
Parrots, Cockatoos, Lorikeets, *Scarlet macaw*

Apodiformes (428)
Hummingbirds, Swifts, *Ruby-throated hummingbird*

Coliiformes (6)
Mousebirds or Colies, *Speckled mousebird*

Caprimulgiformes (105)
Nightjars, Frogmouths, Oilbirds *Spotted nightjar*

Coraciiformes (200)
Bee-eaters, Kingfishers, *Crested kingfisher*

Passeriformes (4,126)
Rooks, Starlings, Finches, Sparrows, Larks, Pipits, Wagtails, Tits, Shrikes, Warblers, Blackbirds, Wrens Thrushes, Robins, Nightingales, Swallows, *House sparrow*

Gaviiformes (4)
Loons or divers, *Red-throated loon*

Piciformes (383)
Woodpeckers, Flickers *Medium-spotted woodpecker*

FAMILY

There is only one family in the order *Gaviiformes*:

Loons

SPECIES

There are four species in the loon family:

Red-throated loon

Arctic loon

Common loon

Yellow Pacific loon

GLOSSARY

Adaptation Special features that help a bird to survive in a particular place. For example, penguins in Antarctica have very thick plumage to keep out the cold.

Aerofoil The name given to the shape of aircraft and bird wings, which are curved on top and flat underneath.

Bill Another word for a bird's beak.

Call A short sound made by a bird to keep a flock together, warn of impending danger, or frighten away intruders.

Camouflage The special colours or markings of a bird's plumage which help it to blend in with its surroundings, and avoid being seen and possibly eaten by predators.

Classification The method scientists use to group together birds that share similar characteristics. To classify birds, scientists look at traits like shape of body and feet, where they nest, and how they feed.

Courtship display The way a bird behaves in order to attract a mate. This may take the form of singing, dancing, or displaying vivid courtship plumage.

Evolution The development of living things into new species which are better adapted to their environment. This takes place over thousands or millions of years; the individual birds that have the best characteristics for their habitat survive and reproduce, while others die out.

Extinction The permanent loss of a species from the planet.

Flock A large or small group of birds that flies together. Many birds migrate in large flocks, often with more than one species.

Habitat The type of place a bird lives in, such as forest, seashore, or desert.

Incubation Eggs have to be kept at about 35°C, so that the chicks inside develop properly. This is called incubation. Most birds sit on their eggs to keep them warm.

Lek A communal display ground where several males of certain species, such as ruffs and grouse, gather to attract females.

Migration A yearly journey, often over a long distance, made by many birds between their summer breeding grounds and their winter feeding grounds.

Moulting The shedding of feathers as they get old and worn out, or are due to be replaced with courtship plumage. Most birds molt once or twice a year.

Nocturnal Birds that are active mainly at night, such as owls. Nocturnal birds have special adaptations for finding their food and their way in the dark.

Pellet The indigestible remains of a bird's meal, such as bones, fur, seed cases, and shells, are regurgitated once or twice a day in the form of tightly-packed pellets.

Plumage A bird's feathers.

Roost The term given to a bird's sleep, and to the place it sleeps, such as a branch. Some birds roost in huge groups.

Song A series of sounds or notes, usually made by a male bird to attract a mate or proclaim ownership of a territory.

Vertebrate An animal with an internal skeleton and a backbone, or spine. Birds, mammals, fish, reptiles, and amphibians are all vertebrates.

Warm-blooded An animal whose internal body temperature stays constant whatever the temperature outside, so it can remain active in warm or cold weather.

INDEX

aerofoil 9, 31
albatross 8
archaeopteryx 4
Arctic tern 11
avocet 13

beaks 12-15, 21, 31
bird of paradise 23, 29
birdcake 14
bird watching 28
bittern 17

call 31
camouflage 7, 19, 24, 26, 31
classification 30, 31
colours 7, 20, 22
communication 30, 31
condor 5
cormorant 9
courtship 22, 23
cuckoo 24

display 23, 31
dove 4
duck 10, 16

eagle 17, 24, 29
eggs 4, 15, 24, 26, 27
emu 8, 9
evolution 4, 22, 31
extinction 4, 8, 13, 15, 31
eyesight 18, 19

feathers 4, 6, 7, 17, 22, 23
feeding 14, 15
feet 16, 17
flamingo 14
flight 4, 5, 7-9

flightless birds 8, 9, 18
flocks 11, 31
frigate bird 14, 22
frogmouth 18

gannet 21
geese 10, 11, 16, 20
guillemot 27

habitat 4, 13, 28, 28, 31
hatching 27
heron 17
hornbill 12
human speech 21
hummingbird 5, 8, 12, 24

incubation 31

jacana 16

kakapo 18
kiwi 9
Kori bustard 5

leks 22, 31
litter 13

macaw 4
migration 10, 11, 20, 31

national birds 29
nest box 25
nest building 24, 25
night birds 18, 19
nightjar 17, 19

oilbird 18
ostrich 5, 8, 16

owl 18, 19, 26

parrot 13, 21
partridge 16
passenger pigeon 15
pelican 5
penguin 9, 21, 26, 28
phoenix 4
plover 26
pollution 13
preening 7
puffin 25

rain forests 28
riflebird 22
roadrunner 29
robin 22
ruff 22
rufous ovenbird 25

scarecrows 15
skeleton 5
smell 12
songs 20-22, 31
spoonbill 13
stomach 15
swan 6

tailorbird 25
talking birds 21
tern 27
toucan 12

village weaver 24

wings 4, 9
woodcock 19
woodpecker 17

Photographic credits:
Cover: top left, top middle and bottom left: Bruce Coleman Limited; top right: Mary Evans Picture Library; bottom right: Roger Vlitos.

Titles page and pages 2, 5 left, 6, 13 top, 15 top and 29 middle and bottom: Roger Vlitos; pages 3 top and 7 middle and bottom right: Robert Harding Picture Library; pages 3 bottom, 4-5 all, 7 top and bottom left, 8 left and right, 10, 12 top and bottom, 14 left and right, 16 top and bottom, 17, 18, 19, 20 top and bottom, 22, 23, top, 24 top, 26, 27, 28 left and right and 29 top: Bruce Coleman Limited; pages 21, 15 bottom and 24 bottom: Planet Earth Pictures; page 23 bottom: Frank Spooner Pictures.